Hello to Me with Love

HELLO TO ME WITH LOVE

Poems of Self-Discovery

by C. Tillery Banks

William Morrow and Company, Inc. New York 1980

Library of Congress Cataloging in Publication Data

Banks, C Tillery.
    Hello to me with love.

    I. Title.
PS3552.A484H4   811'.54   80-111
ISBN 0-688-03623-6

Book Design by Lesley Achitoff

Printed in the United States of America

First Edition
1   2   3   4   5   6   7   8   9   10

My sincerest thanks to everyone who has
touched my life in any way . . .

Hello to Me with Love

Learning
To spend time
With myself
By myself
Liking
My OWN
Company
Conversation
Held singly
Cruising
Inside
ME
Checking
MySELF
out

no more ugly days for me
the sun shines always
and the rain is sweet and cleansing
washing my gutters clean

cloudy days will be soft and hazy
not blue or lonely

problems will only be challenges

and sickness will just be
a signal to listen

Even My Pain's Gonna Be Pretty.

disappointment will be growth
because it will teach me
to choose more carefully

delays will be lessons in patience
because I know everything comes in time
on time
even when I'm late
I'll be
on time

there is no loss
if anything goes
I gave it away
and blessed
whoever
got it

Even My Pain's Gonna Be Pretty.

closed doors are wrong paths
jammed doors will be opened
since I will learn the truth

I'll not be tired
only resting

no mistakes
only lessons
and growth
and change
movement

Joy! Joy! Joy!
    Even My Pain's Gonna Be Pretty.

Glory! Glory! Glory!

    EVEN MY PAIN'S GONNA BE PRETTY.

I don't pretend to understand
        What it is/about you
        Why it is/I accept
The things
You
Do

        Loving-and-hurting
        All-at-the-same-time
        Telling-myself
        This-is-the-last-time

        What is it/What it is?

        You-say-anything-you-feel
        Go-anywhere-you-want-to-go
        See-who-you-want-to-see

And I pretend not to know
Can't face the truth
That
You
        Want to go/Already gone

The look in your eyes is dead
A look my soul has come to dread
      Yet-I-avoid-the-reality
      Of-it-all

      And hang on/Hang on

Tell myself
      Give-it-up-girl
      Move-on-out-into-the-world
      Find-someone-who-will-love-you
      Cast-off-the-old
      And-welcome-the-new

Yeah
        Tomorrow/Tomorrow
But today
You
Get
Your
Way

Time Somebody Told Me

Time somebody told me
  That I am lovely, good and real
  That my beauty could make hearts stand still:

It's Time somebody told me
  That my love is total and so complete
  That my mind is quick and full of wit
  That my lovin is just too good to quit:

Time somebody told me.

Time somebody told me
  How much they want, love and need me
  How much my spirit helps set them free
  How my eyes shine full of the white light
  How good it feels just to hold me tight:

Time Somebody Told Me.

So I had a talk with myself
  just me—nobody else

Cause it *was* time *somebody* told me.

New Direction

I made a change and all was new
The way I loved me
The way I loved you

I made a change/I see the light
No longer does my spirit
Feel uptight

Traveling life's winding road
I no longer carry a heavy load
Feel good/feel happy/feel alive
Can't be stopped by no bullshit jive

Got my eyes on the mark
My feet move toward the light/not the dark

No problem with tomorrow
Cause today is so good
Tomorrow takes care itself
Just the way it should

Got to keep my channels open
To hear that inner voice
That helps me on this journey
Make the right choice

Get still and listen. In silence lie all my answers.

Rhythms of a House

I enter your house
and the rhythm begins
an orderly one it is:
   Smooth, even flowing, calming to the spirit

   Movement called easy
   motion without the disturbance of movement
      soft, silent movement
      accomplishing tasks without effort

   The earthy rhythms
   of the colors
   of your house
      are strong, binding, rooting
      stabilizing the soul and the body

   All in harmony
   meaning absence of discord
      continuous rhythm
      guiding the spirit gently along

      The whispers of the plants
      chanting their life-giving melodies
         renewing the old
         giving birth to the new

   New rhythms
   Old rhythms
   Future rhythms
      Moving me along to good
      For
      Good.

BROWN silky eyes
Flashing stories
at me:
>I try to hide
>from all they say
>But they won't let me
>have my way

SILKY lashes
Flashing love
at me:
>Energy flowing
>from you
>Brings me
>such glee

EYES
Stealing
my secrets:
>Demanding my love
>Seizing my truth
>Making me
>Whole again

BEAUTIFUL
BROWN
SILKY
EYES:
>Don't stop
>Watching
>me.

Missing the warmth
      (of hands gliding over my body)
      (kisses sprinkled lightly)
      (causing my hair to stand on end)
      (and chills to roll)

Missing you
      (calling my name)
      (in that special way)
      (that only you)
      (can call it)

Missing you

      (Missing you.)

You
Me
Us . . .
      Moving towards something
      Caught up in the beauty of our being
      Loving this new way of seeing

Can't get enough
Can't get enough

      Your tongue writes
           love letters in my soul
      Your spirit sings
           me lullabies
      Your fingers tap
           dreams of wonderful possibilities
           throughout my body
      Your being holds
           my promise of a wonderful tomorrow

All I can say is

Hello
and
Welcome . . .

*

*You make
the feel-in'
good.

You make
the feel-in'
good.

Inside.

      You Tip
inside my mind
      Whisper
your love songs
      Ease
inside my essence
      and Sprinkle
Star Joy—

      JUMP
inside my pain
      and SCATTER
the hurt
      and LEAP
inside my body
      filling me
with Liquid Love—

      LIQUIDLOVE
      Running
      Down my legs
      Thru my veins
      From your heart
      To my heart

      FLUID HARMONY
      Filling
      Me
UP

Inside.

Not enough time to say what I could . . .
Not enough skill to say what I would . . .
Not enough space to do what I should . . .
but I love you . . .
and you understand.

it does not matter
how long you stay
forever
is in me
        and i control it.

your beauty
your joy
are mine
to recall
        always
        whenever . . .

your tenderness
is tucked around
the corners
of my heart
        matters not
        if we are
        together
        or apart

your gentleness
wakes me
with a smile
remembering
        all those times
        you held me tight
        all through the night
        remembering . . .

no
it does not matter
how long you stay
i keep you inside me
      in my
      very own
      special
      way

the glow
in your eyes
warms my soul
even after you've gone
to where
whom
or what
the glow
lingers
      and warms
      and warms
      and warms

loving me
does not mean
you can't
love someone
else
won't love
someone else
shouldn't
love
someone else

hopefully
loving me
means
you can
      love
      someone
      else
      better

Don't touch me now!
Just let me be.
      It's not the time
      To start
            Feeling again
            Loving again
            Wanting again.

Don't touch me now!
Just let me be.
      Lonely I know
      It's familiar to me.

            /moving inside me
            touching my heart
            sharing my feelings
            starting a new start/

Don't touch me now!
Just let me be.
        Lonely I know
        It's familiar to me.

                /writing new songs
                soothing old wrongs
                dancing new dances
                taking new chances
                going new places
                finding new spaces/

                please

Don't touch me now!
Just let me be.

                /making me laugh
                till I have to cry
                gently, tenderly
                rocking me sweet
                like a lullaby/
                /traveling inside me
                so I can't hide
                into my center
                where my peace abides/

Leave me alone!
Just let me be.
Leave me alone!
      Go on home
      That's where
      You belong
And let me be
        /let me be/

Don't touch me now.
Just let me be.

Touch and go,
I don't want any more!
So just let me be.
        /let me be/

A door opens
    a new path
    a new hope
    a new joy
Then it closes.
Sadness reigns for a moment.

Then another door opens
    the same path
    —a deeper hope
    —a deeper joy
all leading to oneself.

Cause after all the doors
have opened and closed
there always remains the
      self
    and the
  universal force
that protects us all.

Goodbye
can be a
Hello—
    A chance to be
    A chance to grow
    A chance to see
    A chance to know

Goodbye
Can
Be
a
Hello

Going cold TURKEY on your ass

Get you out
my system
QUICK
I know all this
Sweet Kindness
will leave ME
in a trick

Goin' COLD turkey on your ass

Can't keep waiting
for the phone to ring
Listenin'
for the sound of
YOUR voice
Sayin' words
that make
MY heart sing

GOIN' cold turkey on your ass

Get your SWEET
smell out of
my SKIN
Smell from rubbin'
OUR bodies together
SO GOOD it's got
to be a SIN

      My mind and heart
      just can't
      HANDLE it
      The stuff is
      just TOO
      damn GOOD
      You know how it
      TOUCHES me
      EXCITES me
      HAUNTS me . . .

You know . . .

GOIN' COLD TURKEY ON YOUR ASS

Just because
I fear
it
won't
last

It is not
          important
that you do not
          say
          I thank you
          or
          I love you
          with your voice
anymore

but

I no longer
          see it
          in your eyes
          or
          in your touch

    I need it so.

My Tears Don't Come Cheap Anymore

I don't want to cry anymore
  about somethin that ain't nothin.

The price of my tears comes high now;
They come from a deeper well than before.

  A well filled with knowledge I didn't have before
      filled with visions I have never seen before
      filled with emotions I have never felt before
      secrets I've never known before.

      Filled with children I have yet to birth
      Joys I have yet to live and to give
      Magic I have yet to perform
      Dreams yet to dream
      Songs to sing that have not been sung
      Dances to dance
      And words to rhyme.

The well is deep.

No, my tears don't come cheap anymore.

I.

loving
you
is
like
taking
a
ride
on
a
magic
carpet
    floating thru and among the hills
    and valleys of your being is

extraordinary

leaves
me
high

so
high

i
find

    so much for me there
    so much for the world there
    so much for you

there.

II.

When I scream
My love cries—
    the wells
        (deep, deep
        inside me)

empty into your rivers
    (my rivers,
      the rivers of life)
Relieving us
Nurturing us
And the echoes
From my screams
    leave my body
      and soul vibrating
With love
So much love . . .

III.

when
you
are in
me
and
i
am in
you
it is as if
all
my
knots
come
un
tied

IV.

You make me wish
I could see me
—Thru your eyes

And watching you
Watch me
—Is so lovely

Use to be
when my fuel tank hit
"E"
I could
fill up
at most
any station.

Now
I find
that most-any-station
won't do
anymore.

So I watch
my gauge
more carefully,
Cause
a high-quality-
octane-fuel
is hard
to come by

—And since
that's all
I can
function-on
I must
practice
energy
conservation.

But
when I
Do find
that special
high-quality-
octane-station
I
fill up
and try to get
a certificate
for-a-refill
—If I
can.

Can't
run-on-
watered-down-
cheap-gas
anymore

—Tried it
and my spirit
demands
more.

Got to be
more conservative
now
Cause
I'm telling
you
—a special
high-quality-octane
pump
—is
—hard
to find.

Your eyes

sparkle

with approval

and love

kindness

and joy

sent

from above

pure

and warm

like

a white dove

holding me close

tight

like a glove.

Reflection

The stars shine again
The sun shines again
The moon caresses my spirit
All coming from
YOUR glances
YOUR smiles
YOUR kiss
YOUR touch
YOUR love

YOU
YOU

YOUR love
YOUR touch
YOUR kiss
YOUR smiles
YOUR glances
All coming from
The moon caresses my spirit
The sun shines again
The stars shine again

Sometimes we pray with our tears . . .

Tears of joy, gratitude for so much kindness,
        tenderness and love—

Feeling so comfortable
     so high
     so wide and full

        Thank you

         Bless You

          Love You

You have always been
walking around
the edges
of my life
                    I knew you
                    when I didn't know you
                    Loved you
                    though I hadn't met you
                    Felt you
                    though I never touched you
Today
you walked
past the edges
to my center
and said
            hello

We've come such a long way
in such a short time . . .

Songs in the same key
Verses seem to rhyme
Rhythm
Keeping perfect time.

Inside my soul you came
Took me, Kept me and loved me
without knowing/or so you say.
    I believed you knew,
      but took a chance
And I lost.

Now I'm picking up the pieces
of my person that I gave to you.

Taking her back
Cause you won't take care of her.

Pasting her together
With the love I have left for myself
    Using the pain for glue
    for it's the strongest substance
    I have left
After the love
I had for you.

When it all fits again
you will have
someone new
    Maybe less, maybe more than before
    More for me, maybe more for you
But definitely
More for me.

Cause I've shut that door
to that deep place I let you enter.
    I can't afford the picking up
    and pasting together again
At least
Not anyway soon.

Free Yourself

Let go
of the old hurts
that keep you pinned down
closed in.

Release
the vengeance
that makes you
the victim.

Live
Breathe
New Life
New Hope
New Joys.

Yesterday's sorrows can only make you weak.
Nourish yourself instead
with love and forgiveness—
beginning with yourself.

Let go
and Free Yourself

Fly above it all
And soar in the peacefulness
Of a new found inner space—
That is controlled
By You
For You.

Free Yourself
and Be Happy.

I might be lonely
but I will at least be happy
happy without the

pain of

non-sharing

non-touching

and

non-caring

You will
not
put out my light:
        I am
        will be
        will shine.

My light is meant to shine:
            to warm
            to nourish
            to guide
            and to share.

You will
not
put out my light:
        Lights that shine together
        are more intense
        more powerful.

I desire to shine with other lights:
                for good
                for mankind.

But I
will not
be smothered
or snuffed out
because my light
frightens
you.

Spend the time intensifying your own light
instead of trying to dim mine:
              So that we may
              stand together
              and shine together.

My light comes
from a space
of truth deep within:

                  a place
                  that just
                     is
                  not by design
                  but it is my gift
                  from the universal power
                  that provides us all.

In truth
I did not know how bright it was
did not really care:

                  until today
                  when you tried
                  to shut it off
                  under the guise of
                  "helpful advice."

Please
don't help me anymore:
                         just let me be
                         learn my lessons
                              and
                              glow.

You
will not
put out
my light.

I need a place

a place to go for solace
for nourishment
to be propped up

I need a place
to place my soul
in the warmth
of love
        healing
        soothing
        helping me
through another day

a place
to be understood
a refuge
without
conditions

giving
and
receiving
        not just giving
        and asking
        sometimes begging

I need a place . . .

        sometimes
        my past
        closes in . . .

the smells
the sights

            strange
            strange . . .

flashing
so quickly

            before
            my
            eyes.

You

Suddenly life is so easy because of you-me-us.

>Your smile sends heat
>>to warm an oft lonely body.
>
>Your eyes send energy
>>to lift a sometimes tired spirit.
>
>Your voice sends encouragement
>>to an often times discouraged soul.
>
>Your touch comforts
>>a sometimes aching body.
>
>Your spirit joins
>>and entwines a forever essence—

God, I'm so thankful for you: your-beauty-your-pain-your-joy—

You-you-you

Everything.

Traveling together
Side by side
Can't remember
When I've had
Such a beautiful ride

Traveling on . . .
We turned a corner yesterday
We heard an old song
Sang a new way

Gazed down the road
Saw only light
Shed our needless loads
Let our hearts take flight

Travelin on . . .
Holding hands
Holding hearts
Nothin' seems to
Keep us apart

Matters not
Where our journey ends
It's just so wonderful
Bein' travelin friends

Travelin together
Travelin as one

Loving

Travelin on.

Learning to lift myself higher
Carrying my own space with me
Taking my spirit by the hand
And leading it upward

Being responsible for thoughts
Because they are *my* thoughts
And they live in my mind
—in my heart
—in my soul
—in me
Making Me
And Mine
And Everything

Changed my thinking
Changed my life
And it is *my* life
—for the first time
—now
—and always

Thank you God
For the God
In Me.

DATE DUE

DATE DUE

ILL:#7016363		
due: 08/02/04		
Aug 11, 2004		

Demco, Inc. 38-293